YOUR KNOWLEDGE H

Bibliographic information published by the German National Library:

The German National Library lists this publication in the National Bibliography; detailed bibliographic data are available on the Internet at http://dnb.dnb.de .

Imprint:

Copyright © 2019 GRIN Verlag
Print and binding: Books on Demand GmbH, Norderstedt Germany
ISBN: 9783668961838

This book at GRIN:

https://www.grin.com/document/476745

Anonym

Cloud Architecture. What are the possibilities of cloud computing?

GRIN Verlag

GRIN - Your knowledge has value

Since its foundation in 1998, GRIN has specialized in publishing academic texts by students, college teachers and other academics as e-book and printed book. The website www.grin.com is an ideal platform for presenting term papers, final papers, scientific essays, dissertations and specialist books.

Visit us on the internet:

http://www.grin.com/

http://www.facebook.com/grincom

http://www.twitter.com/grin_com

Software Architectures

Winter semester 2018/2019

Fachhochschule Dortmund

Cloud Architecture

21.12.2018

Digital Transformation M.Sc.

1. Semester

Table of Contents

1 Introduction

The cloud and cloud computing are topics everyone is currently talking about. It is often used as a buzzword in marketing to improve the sales just because it sounds modern. Nevertheless, the cloud is a very important topic in the IT environment nowadays. There are probably still a lot of companies that do not use cloud tools at all or just a small portion of the benefits, simply because they do not know what is possible and what is not possible.

This paper is going to explore the possibilities of cloud computing, which effects different cloud architectures have and in which scenarios they are relevant. First, the basics of cloud computing are explained, how it basically works, and what the standard cloud models are. Afterwards different scenarios for cloud computing and their technological architectures are shown. To display how different cloud architectures can be build, the solutions of OpenStack and OpenNebula for creating a cloud infrastructure are introduced and compared to each other. To frame the paper, the topic will be shortly summarized in the end.

2 Basics of Cloud Computing

Cloud computing is basically serving computing resources of different levels of abstraction, most of the times over the internet using a pay-per-use model. The resources can be concrete resources like storage or networks, but also for example web applications. The target of cloud computing is to reduce the configuration and management expenditure for end users and organizations. Customers of a cloud system have none or only very little setup requirements like installing software. Computational resources should be rapidly scalable, so that usage spikes can be handled with ease and often the resources of a cloud system seem unlimited. Furthermore, concrete resources like storage or processing power should be dynamically assignable, independent of the customer's location (See Brockhaus 2018 and Mell/Grance 2011: 2).

2.1 Service Models of Cloud Computing

There are three common service models of cloud computing.

First, there is Software as a Service (SaaS). When some piece of software is available over the internet, directly targeting the end user, without the need to install anything, it is called Software as a Service. It is usually accessible through various devices e.g. via a web browser. A Software as a Service can consist of one or more small components that can be integrated and used by other applications, e.g. OpenID, or it can be a complete application, like Google Maps or Google Docs (see Baun et al. 2011: 37).

Second, there is Platform as a Service (PaaS). A Platform as a Service is usually not for end users but for software developers. The platform can offer an environment for the developers to program their applications, or it can offer a runtime environment on which the developers can deploy their own applications. A Platform as a Service aims for easy and fast setup, installation and deployment. Customers do not have access to the underlying infrastructure like servers or networks, but they have the complete control over the deployed applications. Some popular examples for Platform as a Service solutions are Google App Engine and Microsoft Azure (see Baun et al. 2011: 35 and Mell/Grance 2011: 2 f.).

Last, there is Infrastructure as a Service (IaaS). An Infrastructure as a Service solution offers an abstract view on hardware, e.g. computing power, storage or networks. The cloud provider offers a user interface to manage all the needed resources. Creation or deletion of operation system images, capacity scaling for computation power or storage, or the definition of network topologies are common use cases. Moreover, the interfaces offer operative functionality for starting and stopping concrete server instances. Depending on the provider, the actual infrastructure can consist of concrete physical hardware, or it can be virtual resources, based on virtualization or containerization. Even though some providers offer a whole range of services, they usually have one main service or technology, e.g. Hadoop MapReduce is used for calculations, Dropbox offers storage, or OpenFlow is used for networking (see Baun et al. 2011: 32 ff.).

An overview of the cloud service models can be seen in Figure 1.

2

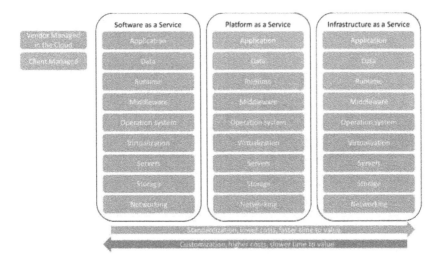

Figure 1: Cloud computing service models (adapted from Schouten 2013)

2.2 Public, Private and Hybrid Clouds

Besides the comparison of the cloud service models, cloud computing systems should be distinguished by their availability to the general public and their distribution.

2.2.1 Public Cloud

If a cloud is available to the public and everyone has the possibility to access it, it is called a public cloud. Public clouds are operated by third party organizations which run and maintain the whole infrastructure. The cloud resources are usually available for any user over the internet. The pricing model is usually pay-per-use for very short time frames, so the users can allocate and free the resources on the fly. This way, they can easily scale their environments and make sure that their services are available all the time. Additionally, companies can reduce their costs for server, as there is no need for additional backup server that are only used at peak times. As the third party vendor is responsible for maintaining the servers, the availability and uptime is usually very high and stable (see Goyal 2014: 23). Examples for public clouds providers are Amazon Web Services (AWS), Microsoft Azure or Google Cloud Platform.

3

The main drawbacks of public clouds are data privacy and security. When data is stored in a public cloud, an organization may not know where the data is stored exactly, how it is backed up, and how secure the data is in terms of accessibility by other people (see Goyal 2014: 23). Especially today, with the General Data Protection Regulation (GDPR) in force, one has to be very careful to make sure that the public cloud is GDPR-compliant when storing sensitive data in the cloud (see Roßnagel et al. 2018: 294). As public clouds are open to everyone, they usually do not reflect the security needs of larger companies, even though they are quite secure in general. Therefore, the usage of a public cloud should be planned very carefully to make sure that the cloud meets all the requirements and does not lead to a new threat for the company. Nevertheless, in smaller companies the security issues can often be considered a benefit instead of a drawback. As they often do not have enough manpower to handle every aspect of security, they could use the public cloud, so they do not have to worry about security for e.g. the data storage (see Goyal 2014: 23).

2.2.2 Private Cloud

A private cloud is, opposed to the public cloud, a cloud that is only available for a single organization or a very small group of connected companies. The functionalities and the data that are made available through the cloud are only used internally, for example to share logistics data between company locations. The private cloud can be operated by the company itself or by a third party organization. Geographically, it is possible to either host it directly at the company, e.g. in their data-center, or at another place, which is less common than the former (see Goyal 2014: 23).

Generally, the usage of a private cloud is not different to the usage of a public cloud. It is also self-service-based, so you can get resources on-demand and the infrastructure is automatically managed by the cloud system. A private cloud is especially interesting if a company has otherwise unused capacities. There might be some servers with very high load and others that idle most of the time. In this scenario, the cloud management software could redistribute the capacities to balance the workload. Another very important advantage is the aspect of security and data privacy. Opposed to the public cloud, a company has all the data as well as the security configurations in their own hands, so they can exactly tell, how secure the data is and where it should be stored (see Goyal 2014: 23).

Even though the private cloud offers a lot of advantages and reduced costs compared to the regular data-centers, it still has disadvantages. Mainly, it is in general more costly than the public cloud as there are the costs for hardware, software, and staff. Furthermore, it is not as flexible as a public cloud. New hardware is required whenever the required calculation power exceeds the available, and there are additional servers to handle traffic spikes (see Goyal 2014: 23).

2.2.3 Hybrid Cloud

Hybrid Clouds combine the advantages of both private and public clouds. One or more private clouds are combined with one or more public clouds to a single, unified system. The clouds are connected via a software system that offers portability of data and functionalities, so the systems can be interconnected. The hybrid cloud is thus usually much more complex than a single private or public cloud (see Goyal 2014: 24).

In a hybrid cloud, some data can be stored inhouse in the private cloud. Usually that would be data which needs high security standards as private data of end users. On the other side, data which does not need specific security treatment can be stored in the public cloud, e.g. data for general statistics. Meanwhile, it is possible to maintain the scalability and cost-effectiveness of a public cloud. When the hybrid cloud system experiences usages spikes, there is no need for additional servers as a buffer, as the overhead can simply be overcome by outsourcing some of the traffic to the public cloud. After the spike, the system just removes the public cloud resources, so the additional costs are minimized (see Goyal 2014: 24).

5

The drawbacks of hybrid clouds are the complexity, and therefore also security issues. A hybrid cloud is not as easy to set up and maintain as a single public or private cloud. It has to be configured and managed carefully to prevent security risks. Additionally, the general security issues of the public cloud are also present. The communication channel between the public and private cloud offers an extended surface for attackers. Hybrid clouds lead to a larger infrastructure and thus more tools in use. These are interesting targets for attackers. For example the hybrid cloud management tool which communicates with all the systems, as it has many external interfaces. Nevertheless, when being implemented thoughtfully, hybrid clouds offer great opportunities and flexibility for different purposes, as there is no standard solution for everyone (see Goyal 2014: 25).

3 Cloud Technologies

Users of cloud services want to make use of computation power, storage, and networking resources. The resources have to be split up dynamically between the participants without disturbing each other. The users want to obtain resources on the fly and at any scale. To cope with this problem, there are different technologies which are going to be discussed in this chapter.

3.1 Virtualization

The major technology used today to handle cloud infrastructures is virtualization. Virtualized environments hide how resources are divided between the servers by offering an abstract view on the overall resources. For consumers, the resources seem to be infinite (see Fox et al. 2009: 2).

Virtualization basically means splitting up one computer in multiple parts, so several operations systems or applications can be executed at the same time. To achieve this, one or more physical hardware systems can be emulated software-sided by one physical computer. It appears like there is more than one physical computer, each with potentially different operation systems and applications running (see Dziak 2018).

6

To achieve the division between the different simulated computers, called virtual machines (VMs), a special piece of software is used to manage these machines – the virtual machine monitor, or more common, hypervisor. The hypervisor handles the hardware resources and coordinates which resources can be accessed by which virtual machine. The hypervisor can either be a minimized operation system that is directly installed on the hardware (type-1 hypervisor), or it can be a dedicated software running on top of a common operation system (type-2 hypervisor). Furthermore, it is differentiated between complete virtualization and para-virtualization. The former simulates a complete computer with every part of it. This approach is quite efficient in terms of computation power, but often lacks network or storage performance. The latter does not emulate hardware, but only offers an application programming interface for the guest operation system. Therefore, the mounted operation system must be individualized to use this interface. This approach is often used for applications that have a lot of storage and network throughput. Examples for complete virtualization hypervisors are KVM or VMware. For Para-virtualization Xen is used commonly (see Baun et al. 2011: 14 f. and Marinescu 2013: 383 f.).

Virtualization can be used not only to run different operation systems and applications (server virtualization), but it can also be used to virtualize networks, storage and desktops. Network virtualization means the simulation of physical networks. This can be for example emulating a network on a single physical machine to connect different virtualized machine with each other. Storage emulation is about publishing data from different source in a unified way and then made available to specific set of users. Finally, desktop virtualization enables different devices to connect to one standardized virtual desktop, so every device can access the same set of tools and applications from various locations (see Dziak 2018).

3.2 VMware ESXi

VMware ESXi is a special kind of hypervisor because it is a bare-metal hypervisor that is directly installed on the physical hardware (see VMware, Inc 2018a). Bare-metal and bare-metal servers are synonyms for physical, non-virtualized servers (see Yamato 2015: 229). ESXi is efficient, because it has direct access to and control of the resources of the bare-metal server, opposed to normal hypervisors which work on top of an operation system. Therefore, the hardware can be used more efficiently. ESXi offers features like a high security standard, good support for different server environments and a user-friendly graphical interface, as well as one for the command line. As a drawback, it is a proprietary hypervisor by VMware and servers running ESXi usually have to be managed by another server running VMware vCenter as server management software (see VMware, Inc 2018a).

3.3 Containerization

Another method of deploying applications or infrastructure are containers. Containerization is a kind of virtualization that is more lightweight than hypervisor-based virtualization. Containers work on a different level of abstraction than hypervisors, as the containers are only virtualizing the operation system and not the whole hardware, which results in a lesser overhead. Containers share the operation system kernel of the host machine. This results in smaller image sizes on the disk and the ability to run a large number of containers at the same time. Even though there are many advantages, containers have the general disadvantage that due to the shared kernel they are not as secure as virtual machines (see Morabito et al. 2015: 1 f.).

4 Scenarios of Cloud Computing

Cloud computing is used in many companies worldwide to improve the development and deployment of applications, but how can you use cloud computing in practice on the market? In this chapter, I will discuss some scenarios of cloud computing and introduce some companies and their cloud architectures.

4.1 Netflix

The first popular example of a company relying on cloud services is the video on-demand platform Netflix. Netflix is a complete Software as a Service solution, as the customers only get a simple overlay, but the whole data and application logic is stored and executed on the servers of Netflix.

Netflix is one of the pioneers of cloud computing, as they began relatively early, in 2008, to migrate their monolithic application to a microservices based application that can be deployed in the cloud. They took this step to decouple their teams from each other, so they can work on the different parts each in their own pace, and to speed up the whole process of deploying the application in either test or production environments (see Netflix Technology Blog 2016). That time, they still had their own physical servers running, but one year later in 2009 they started to completely migrate their system to the IaaS of Amazon Web Services.

In short, the reasons for Netflix to use cloud computing were

- scalability without having to reimplement the whole data center,
- the focus on development and not infrastructure,
- the difficulty of estimation of future growth,
- and the general belief in cloud computing

(see Bukoski et al. 2010).

4.2 Salesforce

Another example of viable usage of cloud computing is the company salesforce. Salesforce offers a customer relationship management (CRM) solution for organizations of all sizes. The CRM system has a lot of features for different topics like customer-service or marketing. The service is subscription based with different levels and features (see Salesforce 2018a). Salesforce offers mainly a Software as a Service. As a user, you simply subscribe to their product and instantly get access to all the tools and functionality through a web application. Salesforce decided to use this model amongst

9

other things, to make the software better available for their customers, make it more flexible and scalable, to profit from easier update mechanisms, and to be able to react faster to the feedback of customers (see Salesforce 2018b and Salesforce 2018c). Furthermore, salesforce runs a Platform as a Service, the "Salesforce Platform". This platform can be used to develop applications like web applications or smartphone apps and it offers APIs to connect external data sources to salesforce (see Salesforce 2018d and Salesforce 2018e). The external data connections are manly used to allow companies to migrate to the salesforce system without having to migrate or lose their data (see Salesforce 2018f). The application integration is used to enhance the user experience, by using salesforce features to create user interfaces, or include community feedback applications. Meanwhile, it is possible to gather the usage data and include it directly in the salesforce system (see Salesforce 2018g). As some extraordinary example to demonstrate the power of the API, it is possible to integrate salesforce data in the game Minecraft (see Trailhead n.d.).

In summary, the platform is used by the customer companies of salesforce to enhance their own experience of the salesforce system, to gain additional functionalities, and to collect more information about the user's behavior.

As you can see, it is completely possible and often efficient to use the cloud computing models connected. In the example of salesforce there is no information about whether they are using an Infrastructure as a Service internally, but it is possible that they do it, as it is a very efficient solution. In generally you can say, that a company can either use a single model for its specific purpose in their cloud architecture, so it can benefit from the specific advantages. Nevertheless, it is highly recommended to use more than one cloud model at once as they reinforce each other. Especially an Infrastructure as a Service model, when used internally, offers a solid foundation for development and production environment for each of the other models.

5 Implementation of a Cloud Architecture

The question many organizations may have is: how can we create our own cloud? There are several different tools on the market to achieve this. In this chapter, I will explain two popular software solutions to implement a cloud architecture in an organization: OpenStack and OpenNebula. After introducing them and highlighting the differences, I will continue by explaining, how Docker can be integrated in a cloud system using OpenStack and OpenNebula, and which advantages can result by using it in the cloud architecture.

5.1 OpenStack

OpenStack is an open source software capable of creating private as well as public clouds. OpenStack can control the whole cloud environment: computing, storage, and networking resources. This can all be managed by an administrator via a dashboard or the OpenStack API and it allows users to get the resources through a web interface. The community consist of several developers working with the users and companies to improve the software further (see Openstack.org 2018a).

5.2 OpenNebula

OpenNebula is a software to manage virtualization in a data center and to build private clouds as well as hybrid cloud solutions. It is often used to optimize data centers through virtualization, so that computing, storage, and networking resources are used efficiently. OpenNebula has full control over the physical and virtual resources to provide features like high availability or capacity management. Furthermore, users can benefit from additional features like self-service.

OpenNebula can also be used on top of already existing infrastructure management solutions like VMware vCenter. This way, cloud features can be used without having to change the basis, so the already familiar tools can stay the same. Features like flexible service provisioning or the connection of in-house infrastructure to a public cloud to create a hybrid system are very interesting in this scenario (see OpenNebula: 2018f).

5.3 Comparison

Even though both ideas try to solve the same basic problem, the implementation is very different.

5.3.1 Basics

First, both solutions are open source solutions that enable the user to create a cloud. They have large communities of developers and users that work on the software and improve it further. Everyone has access to the code repositories and can contribute something. This makes the software quite robust.

Furthermore, they both support all three types of cloud: public, private and hybrid cloud, even though they have a different focus. OpenStack focuses more on enterprises, whilst OpenNebula is suitable for a larger spectrum (see Wen et al. 2012: 2461). The support for different operation systems of their hosts is quite large, they support the migration of virtual machines to between different physical servers (virtual machine migration), and both offer an interface to public cloud systems like Amazon Web Services (see OpenStack.org 2018g and OpenNebula.org n.d.).

5.3.2 Administration

Both systems have on the one hand an administration interface for the command line as well as a graphical interface. On the other hand, they also provide an interface for the end users, so they can easily access the resources provided. The graphical user interface is in both systems not a part of the core system, but it can be added to the system with no trouble (see OpenStack.org 2018g and OpenNebula.org 2018g).

5.3.3 Popularity and Distribution

OpenNebula and OpenStack have grown quite diverse. OpenNebula is older than OpenStack. OpenNebula version 1.0 was published on 24.07.2008, whereas OpenStack was published by the end of 2010 (see OpenStack.org 2018d and OpenNebula.org 2018h).

Nevertheless, OpenStack seems to be more popular. As of Google Trends the search term "OpenStack" seems to be much more popular than the search term "OpenNebula" (see Google 2018). Also, as of Wen et al. 2012: 2459 f., OpenStack got a lot more attention since it was published until 2012.

When looking at the organizations that use each software, both of them have a variety of large and popular organizations as users. OpenStack has more of the "big players" in the industry, like HP, Dell, Cisco or IBM as their userbase, whereas OpenNebula seems to be much more popular in the scientific context, as there are many universities and scientific companies that use OpenNebula, for example the Harvard University or the NASA (see OpenNebula 2018e and Openstack.org 2018c).

5.3.4 Architecture

The architectural styles of OpenStack and OpenNebula are very different.

OpenStack's architecture is component based and very modular. There are different components for all functions the OpenStack cloud has to offer, so the user can just pick the thinks he likes to and does not have to handle anything else. There is for example "Nova" for virtual machine computing, "Keystone" for identity management, or "Horizon" as dashboard. This architecture is good if you want to have a highly configurable cloud and there are also some sample configurations, but it could be overwhelming if you first get into contact with the system (see Openstack.org 2018a and Openstack.org 2018f). An overview of the components of OpenStack is shown in Figure 2.

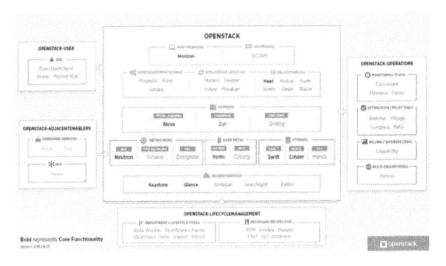

Figure 2: OpenStack component map (adapted from OpenStack 2018g)

The architecture of OpenNebula is simpler than the one of OpenStack. OpenNebula has its main functionality bundled and is only extendable via plug-ins. Even though the main functionality is split in components logically, it is not possible to choose from a variety of options as in OpenStack. Nevertheless, OpenNebula supports many different services via their add-on system.

OpenNebula offers two different architectures to choose from.

The first is the "Open Cloud Architecture", which is the default option if there is no already existing system. For the virtual machines, this architecture depends on the Kernel-based Virtual Machine (KVM) hypervisor natively, but it is also possible to interact with different hypervisors. It uses plain datastores to store the images and disks of the virtual machines and it has a basic networking and authentication layer. Once the cloud is running, there is a number of advanced components like the public cloud functionality or a monitoring service (see OpenNebula.org 2018a).

The second architecture is the "VMware Cloud Architecture". As the name suggests, it is using the stack of VMware and is made especially for organizations that already

14

have an existing VMware infrastructure and do not want to renew their entire software stack. OpenNebula seamlessly integrate with the VMware solutions like vCenter or vSphere. In this configuration it is possible to use the whole tooling of VMware, their workflows, and their procedures while having the ability to use OpenNebula to use advanced cloud features like a connection to the public cloud (see OpenNebula.org 2017).

5.3.5 Hypervisors

The support for different hypervisors is better in OpenStack. OpenStack can use more than one hypervisor at once by using specific filters, but it is generally recommended to choose only one. The support hypervisors are as of OpenStack.org 2018e:

- Kernel-based Virtual Machine (KVM)
- Linux Containers (LXC)
- Quick EMUlator (QEMU)
- User Mode Linux (UML)
- VMware vSphere
- Xen (using libvirt)
- XenServer
- Hyper-V
- Virtuzzo

OpenNebula only supports two hypervisors natively. These are KVM and the VMware hypervisor. Additionally, in the ecosystem there is support for Hyper-V, OpenVZ and VirtualBox (see OpenNebula.org n.d. a and OpenNebula 2017).

5.3.6 Integration of ESXi

Both OpenStack as well as OpenNebula support the usage of ESXi cluster in their cloud computing models.

In OpenStack, the computing module "Nova" has a driver for VMware vCenter to communicate with and manage ESXi hosts. It works in the way that the computing

15

module first clusters the ESXi hosts and after that only communicates through vCenter instances, which act as large hypervisors for the individual clusters. The basic architecture is shown in Figure 3. It is not possible to access the ESXi hosts individually, only the clusters as a whole. When running more than one ESXi cluster, it is advised to run the same number of nova-computing services, so that the scheduling stays efficient (see OpenStack 2018b).

It should also be mentioned that VMware offers a specialized OpenStack distribution called "VMware Integrated OpenStack". This is a deployment-ready solution that is completely built for the VMware stack and works with ESXi out of the box (see VMware, Inc 2018b).

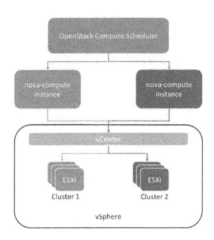

Figure 3: VMware ESXi Architecture (adapted from OpenStack 2018b)

OpenNebula supports ESXi clusters out of the box in the VMware Cloud Architecture. The system here works very equally to the one of OpenStack. It is expected, that the ESXi hosts are clustered and managed by a vCenter instance. OpenNebula has vCenter drivers that act as aggregated hypervisors for the ESXi clusters, just like the nova-compute instances. In OpenNebula it is also not possible to access single ESXi instances but only the whole cluster (see OpenNebula 2017).

5.4 Integration of Docker

Containerization, or container-based virtualization, especially with Docker is a very important aspect in the architecture of a modern cloud. Docker makes the cloud even more flexible than the "legacy" virtualization methods. Docker is a very high-level platform for containers that is made to improve the portability and deployment frequency of applications, has a large tooling ecosystem and increases the ability to automate processes.

The docker images can be run nested inside other virtual machines, or they can be run directly on top of some basic host operation system of a physical server (see Morabito et al. 2015: 387 and Docker Inc. 2018a). When using Docker in a nest virtualization environment, so that the Docker container is running inside a virtual machine, the performance may be decreased, as the server must execute the virtualization layer as overhead. Additionally, running a container does not offer any benefit and can mean introduction of a security risk (see Felter et al. 2015: 172). As an example, in Lubomski et al. 2018 there is a nested system in use, where Docker runs on top of a Debian operation system which runs on a virtual machine via ESXi. In this case the Docker layer does not have a significant performance impact, but the virtualization layer impacts the performance on the networking level (see Lubomski et al. 2018).

Docker, or in general container solutions, have a very good integration in OpenStack as well as OpenNebula.

In the official OpenStack documentation, it is stated that virtual machines do not meet the needs of an agile approach. Even though they are much more flexible than bare-metal servers, they only serve as a foundation. With the container technology whole applications can be easily deployed without having to install anything manually as all the dependencies are packed in the image.

In OpenStack it is possible to run and manage bare-metals servers, virtual machines and containers together. This approach is very comfortable when you still have to manage legacy infrastructure and applications. OpenStack is specialized for container orchestration[1] and works very well with the container orchestration engine (COE) Kubernetes.

There are three different advised scenarios for using containers in OpenStack.

The first one is the usage of infrastructure containers. Here, the cloud infrastructure is improved by using containers for deployment, management and operation of the cloud. The containers run natively on bare-metal servers and have direct access to the resources of them, so they can access to computing, storage and network resources. It is easy to set up and especially good if the hardware is likely to change in the future, as the containers can be deployed hardware independent. Even OpenStack itself can be run on containers to make it easier to upgrade or add new components.

The second approach is the hosting of containerized application frameworks. Container orchestration engines can be set up on OpenStack so that containers can directly be deployed in the system. The containers can be hosted on bare-metal servers, as well as nested inside other virtual machines. In the end, these containers help people to develop, test and deploy applications in an OpenStack context rapidly.

The last scenario is the usage of containers to enhance applications using the OpenStack components. The applications running in COEs on OpenStack can have access to the OpenStack drivers, so the applications can use the functionalities of OpenStack, like the storage system or load-balancing. For example, Kubernetes can be attached to OpenStack to use its hosted volumes (Cinder) or the authorization (Keystone) (see Openstack.org 2018h and Ahn et al. n.d.).

OpenNebula has a built-in Docker integration, but to create hosts where Docker containers can be deployed on it is needed to install the OpenNebula Docker appliance first. Docker enables OpenNebula to manage and provide hosts in a simple way.

---

[1] Coordination of container-based, virtualized services (see Tosatto et al. 2015: 70)

There are three ways for the end user to make use of the Docker instances. The easiest approach is the usage of the built-in tools of OpenNebula. You can simply use the OpenNebula graphical user interface or command line tools to instantiate and manage the Docker containers (see OpenNebula.org 2018b).

It is also possible to run the containers by using the Docker Machine driver for OpenNebula, which is included in the Docker appliance. When using this scenario, you just use the default docker-machine command, which is default tool for handling remote Docker hosts, provided directly by Docker (Docker Inc. 2018b). It is possible to either use images that are based on vanilla operation systems that are supported by Docker, or to use boot2docker for OpenNebula images. These are specialized images that have all packages needed to be run on OpenNebula already packed with then, so they boot faster than the vanilla[2] images. Using Docker Machine, it is also possible to manage the Docker hosts remote (see OpenNebula.org 2016, OpenNebula.org 2018c and OpenNebula.org 2018d).

The third and last approach is simply using the Docker client to execute commands on the remote host (see OpenNebula.org 2018b).

6 Conclusion

This paper gave a brief overview of the topic of cloud architecture including the basic concepts and technological aspects. Some real-life scenarios of enterprises using the cloud were discussed. In the end two popular tools to implement a cloud architecture in organizations were described, as well as their advantages and disadvantages.

In the end, cloud architectures are used to improve the speed and quality of software development and deployment by enabling scalability and reliability without having to worry about the actual hardware. It opens new possibilities for software systems and is definitely a topic that has future relevance.

---

[2] Basic; without any changes (see Cambridge University Press 2018)

19

7 List of figures

8 Bibliography

Ahn, Jaesuk; Berendt, Christian; Bertucio, Anne; Birley, Pete; Hoge, Chris; Kong, Lingxian et al. (n.d.): Leveraging Containers and OpenStack. A Comprehensive Review. Available online at https://www.openstack.org/containers/leveraging-containers-and-openstack/, checked on 20.12.2018.

Baun, Christian; Kunze, Marcel; Nimis, Jens; Tai, Stefan (2011): Cloud Computing. Berlin, Heidelberg: Springer Berlin Heidelberg.

Brockhaus (2018). In: Brockhaus Enzyklopädie Online: NE GmbH | Brockhaus. Available online at http://brockhaus.de/ecs/enzy/article/cloud-computing checked on 21.12.2018.

Bukoski, Ed; McGarr, Mike; Moyles, Brian (2010): Four Reasons We Choose Amazon's Cloud as Our Computing Platform. Netflix Technology Blog. Available online at https://medium.com/netflix-techblog/how-we-build-code-at-netflix-c5d9bd727f15, updated on 14.12.2010, checked on 20.12.2018.

Cambridge University Press (2018): Definition of "vanilla". Cambridge Advanced Learner's Dictionary & Thesaurus. Available online at https://dictionary.cambridge.org/dictionary/english/vanilla, checked on 21.12.2018.

Docker Inc. (2018a): Docker frequently asked questions (FAQ). Available online at https://docs.docker.com/engine/faq, checked on 20.12.2018.

Docker Inc. (2018b): Docker Machine Overview. What is Docker Machine? Available online at https://docs.docker.com/machine/overview/#what-is-docker-machine, checked on 20.12.2018.

Dziak, Mark (2018): Virtualization (computing). In Salem Press Encyclopedia. Available online at https://widgets.ebscohost.com/prod/customerspecific/s9218820/vpn/vpn_fhdo.php?url=http://search.ebscohost.com/login.aspx?direct=true&db=ers&AN=109057164&lang=de&site=eds-live&scope=site.

Felter, Wes; Ferreira, Alexandre; Rajamony, Ram; Rubio, Juan (2015): An updated performance comparison of virtual machines and Linux containers. In IEEE International Symposium on Performance Analysis of Systems and Software. Philadelphia, PA, USA, 29.03.2015 - 31.03.2015: IEEE, pp. 171–172.

Fox, Armando; Griffith, Rean; Joseph, Anthony; Katz, Randy; Konwinski, Andrew; Lee, Gunho et al. (2009): Above the clouds: A berkeley view of cloud computing. In Dept. Electrical Eng. and Comput. Sciences, University of California, Berkeley, Rep. UCB/EECS 28 (13), p. 2009.

Google (2018): Google Trends. opennebula, openstack. Available online at https://trends.google.de/trends/explore?date=all&q=opennebula,openstack, checked on 20.12.2018.

Goyal, Sumit (2014): Public vs Private vs Hybrid vs Community - Cloud Computing: A Critical Review. In *IJCNIS* 6 (3), pp. 20–29. DOI: 10.5815/ijcnis.2014.03.03.

Lubomski, Paweł; Kalinowski, Andrzej; Krawczyk, Henryk (2016): Multi-level Virtualization and Its Impact on System Performance in Cloud Computing. In *Communications in Computer and Information Science* 608, pp. 247–259. DOI: 10.1007/978-3-319-39207-3_22.

Marinescu, Dan C. (2013): Cloud Computing. Theory and Practice. Amsterdam: Morgan Kaufmann/Elsevier (Safari Tech Books Online). Available online at http://gbv.eblib.com/patron/FullRecord.aspx?p=1213925.

Mell, P. M.; Grance, T. (2011): The NIST Definition of Cloud Computing. Recommendations of the National Institute of Standards and Technology. Edited by National Institute of Standards and Technology. National Institute of Standards and Technology.

Morabito, Roberto; Kjallman, Jimmy; Komu, Miika (2015 - 2015): Hypervisors vs. Lightweight Virtualization: A Performance Comparison. In : 2015 IEEE International Conference on Cloud Engineering. 2015 IEEE International Conference on Cloud Engineering (IC2E). Tempe, AZ, USA, 09.03.2015 - 13.03.2015: IEEE, pp. 386–393.

Netflix Technology Blog (2016): How We Build Code at Netflix. Available online at https://medium.com/netflix-techblog/how-we-build-code-at-netflix-c5d9bd727f15, updated on 09.03.2016, checked on 20.12.2018.

OpenNebula.org (n.d.): OpenNebual Frequently Asked Questions. Which hypervisors can OpenNebula use? Available online at https://opennebula.org/about/faq/ #toggle-id-8, checked on 19.12.2018.

OpenNebula.org (2016): OpenNebula Marketplace. boot2docker. Available online at http://marketplace.opennebula.systems/appliance/56d073858fb81d0315000002, updated on 26.02.2016, checked on 20.12.2018.

OpenNebula.org (2017): VMware Cloud Architecture. Available online at http://docs.opennebula.org/5.6/deployment/cloud_design/vmware_cloud_architecture.html, updated on 14.06.2017, checked on 20.12.2018.

OpenNebula.org (2018a): Open Cloud Architecture. Available online at http://docs.opennebula.org/5.6/deployment/cloud_design/open_cloud_architecture.html, updated on 17.12.2018, checked on 20.12.2018.

OpenNebula.org (2018b): Applications Containerization. Overview. Available online at http://docs.opennebula.org/5.6/advanced_components/applications_containerization/overview.html, updated on 16.05.2018, checked on 20.12.2018.

OpenNebula.org (2018c): Docker Machine OpenNebula Driver. Available online at Docker Machine OpenNebula Driver, updated on 24.01.2018, checked on 20.12.2018.

OpenNebula.org (2018d): Applications Containerization. Docker Hosts Provision with Docker Machine. Available online at http://docs.opennebula.org/5.6/advanced_components/applications_containerization/docker_host_provision_with_docker_machine.html, updated on 16.05.2018, checked on 20.12.2018.

OpenNebula.org (2018e): OpenNebula Users. Available online at https://opennebula.org/featuredusers/, checked on 20.12.2018.

OpenNebula.org (2018f): OpenNebula Key Features. Available online at https://opennebula.org/key-features/, checked on 20.12.2018.

OpenNebula.org (2018g): Sunstone Setup. Overview. Available online at https://docs.opennebula.org/5.6/deployment/sunstone_setup/overview.html, checked on 21.12.2018.

OpenNebula.org (2018h): Release Cycle. Available online at https://opennebula.org/release/, updated on 11.10.2018, checked on 20.12.2018.

Openstack.org (2018a): What is OpenStack? Available online at https://www.openstack.org/software/, checked on 20.12.2018.

Openstack.org (2018b): VMware vSphere. Available online at https://docs.openstack.org/ocata/config-reference/compute/hypervisor-vmware.html, updated on 15.08.2018, checked on 20.12.2018.

Openstack.org (2018c): The World #RunsOnOpenStack. Available online at https://www.openstack.org/user-stories, checked on 20.12.2018.

Openstack.org (2018d): OpenStack Releases. Available online at https://releases.openstack.org/, updated on 20.12.2018, checked on 20.12.2018.

Openstack.org (2018e): Hypervisors. Available online at https://docs.openstack.org/ocata/config-reference/compute/hypervisors.html, updated on 15.08.2018, checked on 20.12.2018.

Openstack.org (2018f): Sample Configurations. Available online at https://www.openstack.org/software/sample-configs, checked on 20.12.2018.

Openstack.org (2018g): OpenStack Overview. Available online at https://www.openstack.org/assets/software/projectmap/openstack-map.pdf, checked on 20.12.2018.

Openstack.org (2018h): Docker. Available online at https://wiki.open-stack.org/wiki/Docker#What_unique_ad-vantages_Docker_bring_over_other_containers_technologies, checked on 20.12.2018.

Roßnagel, Alexander; Friedewald, Michael; Hansen, Marit (Eds.) (2018): Die Fortentwicklung des Datenschutzes. Zwischen Systemgestaltung und Selbstregulierung. Wiesbaden: Springer Fachmedien Wiesbaden (DuD-Fachbeiträge). Available online at http://dx.doi.org/10.1007/978-3-658-23727-1.

Salesforce (2018a): Produkte. Available online at https://www.salesforce.com/de/products/, checked on 20.12.2018.

Salesforce (2018b): Was ist SaaS? Available online at https://www.salesforce.com/de/learning-centre/tech/saas, checked on 20.12.2018.

Salesforce (2018c): Service Cloud – Preisübersicht. Available online at https://www.salesforce.com/de/editions-pricing/service-cloud/, checked on 20.12.2018.

Salesforce (2018d): Salesforce Platform. Was ist die Salesforce Platform? Available online at https://www.salesforce.com/de/products/platform/overview/, checked on 20.12.2018.

Salesforce (2018e): Salesforce Platform. Welche Möglichkeiten bietet mir die Salesforce Platform? Available online at https://www.salesforce.com/de/products/platform/solutions/, checked on 20.12.2018.

Salesforce (2018g): Engere Kundenbeziehungen durch Mobile Apps. Available online at https://www.salesforce.com/de/products/platform/solutions/build-customer-experiences/, checked on 20.12.2018.

Salesforce (2018f): Lightning Platform. Integration. Available online at https://www.salesforce.com/products/platform/services/how-you-integrate/, checked on 20.12.2018.

Schouten, Edwin (2013): IBM SmartCloud essentials. Navigate and use the IBM SmartCloud portfolio for building cloud solutions. Birmingham, UK: Packt Pub (Professional expertise distilled). Available online at http://proquest.tech.safari-booksonline.de/9781782170648.

Trailhead (n.d.): Understand the Salesforce Architecture. Available online at https://trailhead.salesforce.com/en/content/learn/modules/starting_force_com/starting_understanding_arch, checked on 20.12.2018.

VMware, Inc (2018a): ESXi. VMware ESXi: The Purpose-Built Bare Metal Hypervisor. Available online at https://www.vmware.com/products/esxi-and-esx.html, checked on 09.12.2018.

VMware, Inc (2018b): VMware Integrated OpenStack. Available online at https://www.vmware.com/products/openstack.html, checked on 20.12.2018.

Wen, Xiaolong; Gu, Genqiang; Li, Qingchun; Gao, Yun; Zhang, Xuejie (2012): Comparison of open-source cloud management platforms: OpenStack and OpenNebula. Piscataway, NJ: IEEE. Available online at http://ieeexplore.ieee.org/servlet/opac?punumber=6227654.

Yamato, Yoji (2015): OpenStack hypervisor, container and Baremetal servers performance comparison. In *IEICE ComEX* 4 (7), pp. 228–232. DOI: 10.1587/comex.4.228.

YOUR KNOWLEDGE HAS VALUE